JINGLE JAZZ

— PIANO LEVEL —
LATE INTERMEDIATE/EARLY ADVANCED

ISBN 978-0-634-03278-3

HAL•LEONARD®
CORPORATION

7777 W. BLUEMOUND RD. P.O. BOX 13819 MILWAUKEE, WI 53213

For all works contained herein:
Unauthorized copying, arranging, adapting, recording or public performance is an infringement of copyright.
Infringers are liable under the law.

Visit Hal Leonard Online at
www.halleonard.com

PREFACE

The lush harmonies of jazz and the rich traditions of Christmas seem to go together well. Many of these popular Christmas songs were originally penned with jazz colorings; others have been dressed up a bit for the occasion.

Most of these melodies have been recorded countless times, yet many are still strongly connected to a particular artist. "The Christmas Song" belongs to Nat King Cole. "Merry Christmas, Darling" is a Carpenters classic. "Feliz Navidad" will always bring Jose Feliciano to mind. "A Merry Christmas to Me" is a new song for the season, a special stocking-stuffer from me to you.

So…light a fire in the fireplace, turn down the lights (except for the piano lamp) and let it snow!

With best holiday wishes,
Phillip Keveren

◆

BIOGRAPHY

Phillip Keveren, a multi-talented keyboard artist and composer, has composed original works in a variety of genres from piano solo to symphonic orchestra. Mr. Keveren gives frequent concerts and workshops for teachers and their students in the United States, Canada, Europe, and Asia. Mr. Keveren holds a B.M. in composition from California State University Northridge and a M.M. in composition from the University of Southern California.

CONTENTS

CAROLING, CAROLING

Words by WIHLA HUTSON
Music by ALFRED BURT
Arranged by Phillip Keveren

TRO - © Copyright 1954 (Renewed) and 1957 (Renewed) Hollis Music, Inc., New York, NY
This arrangement © Copyright 2001 Hollis Music, Inc., New York, NY
International Copyright Secured
All Rights Reserved Including Public Performance For Profit
Used by Permission

THE CHRISTMAS SONG
(CHESTNUTS ROASTING ON AN OPEN FIRE)

Music and Lyric by MEL TORME
and ROBERT WELLS
Arranged by Phillip Keveren

Expressive Ballad

© 1946 (Renewed) EDWIN H. MORRIS & COMPANY, A Division of MPL Communications, Inc.
This arrangement © 2001 EDWIN H. MORRIS & COMPANY, A Division of MPL Communications, Inc.
All Rights Reserved

CHRISTMAS TIME IS HERE

Words by LEE MENDELSON
Music by VINCE GUARALDI
Arranged by Phillip Keveren

Copyright © 1966 LEE MENDELSON FILM PRODUCTIONS, INC.
Copyright Renewed
This arrangement Copyright © 2001 LEE MENDELSON FILM PRODUCTIONS, INC.
International Copyright Secured   All Rights Reserved

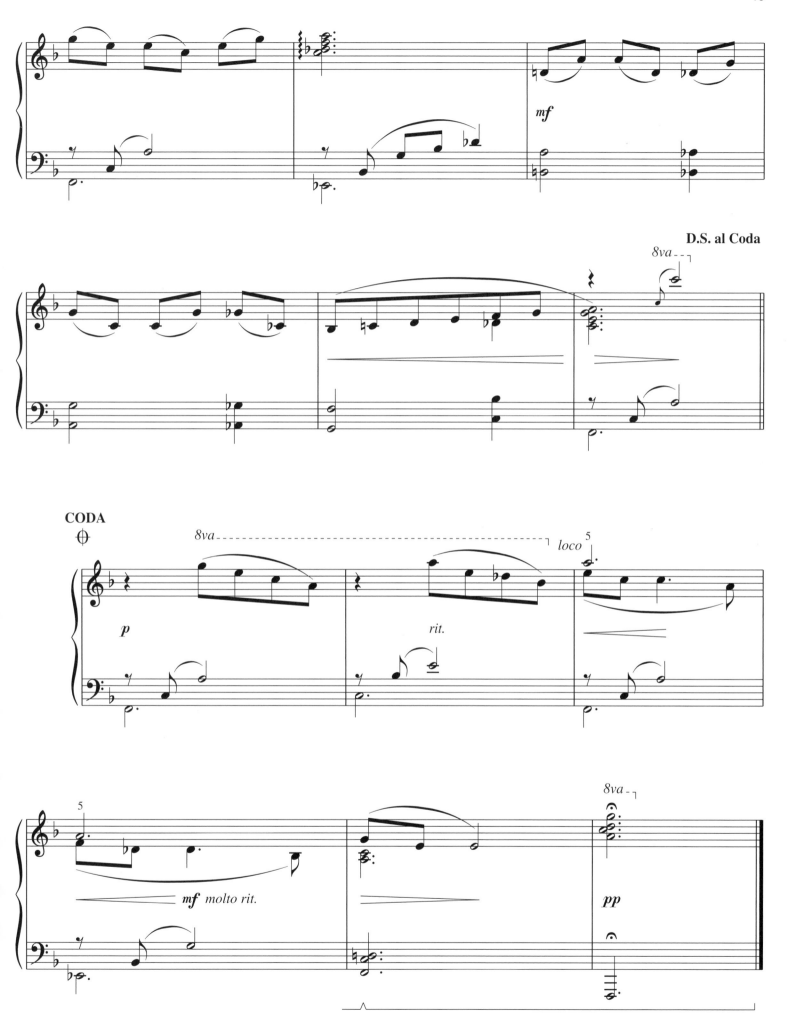

THE CHRISTMAS WALTZ

Words by SAMMY CAHN
Music by JULE STYNE
Arranged by Phillip Keveren

Rubato, with nostalgia

Copyright © 1954 by Producers Music Publishing Co. and Cahn Music Co.
Copyright Renewed
This arrangement Copyright © 2001 by Producers Music Publishing Co. and Cahn Music Co.
All Rights for Producers Music Publishing Co. Administered by Chappell & Co.
All Rights for Cahn Music Co. Administered by WB Music Corp.
International Copyright Secured   All Rights Reserved

FELIZ NAVIDAD

Music and Lyrics by
JOSE FELICIANO
Arranged by Phillip Keveren

Festively Latin

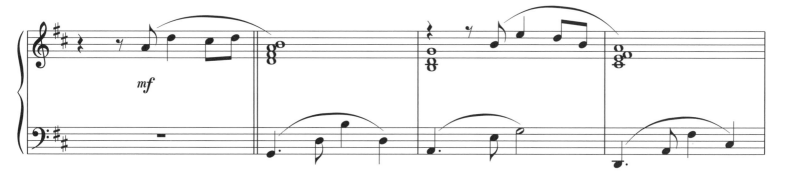

Copyright © 1970 J & H Publishing Company (ASCAP)
Copyright Renewed
This arrangement Copyright © 2001 J & H Publishing Company (ASCAP)
All Rights Administered by Stollman and Stollman o/b/o J & H Publishing Company
International Copyright Secured   All Rights Reserved

(THERE'S NO PLACE LIKE)
HOME FOR THE HOLIDAYS

Words by AL STILLMAN
Music by ROBERT ALLEN
Arranged by Phillip Keveren

Warmly, freely

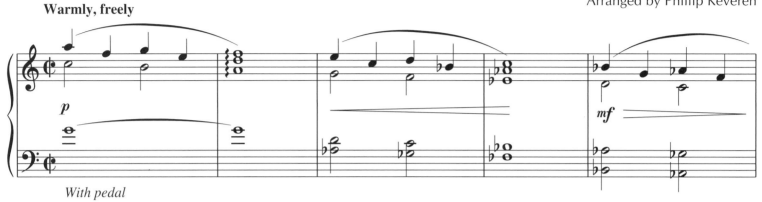

With pedal

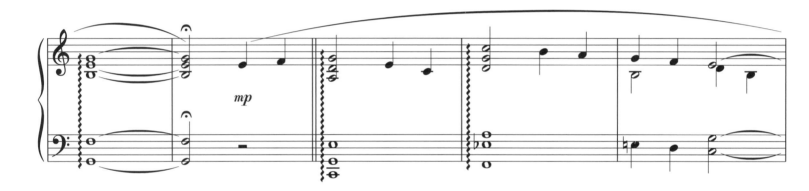

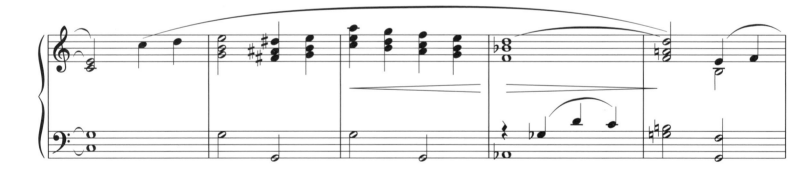

© Copyright 1954 Roncom Music Co.
Copyright Renewed 1982 and Assigned to Charlie Deitcher Productions, Inc. and Kitty Anne Music Co.
This arrangement © Copyright 2001 Charlie Deitcher Productions, Inc. and Kitty Anne Music Co.
International Copyright Secured   All Rights Reserved

I'LL BE HOME FOR CHRISTMAS

Words and Music by KIM GANNON
and WALTER KENT
Arranged by Phillip Keveren

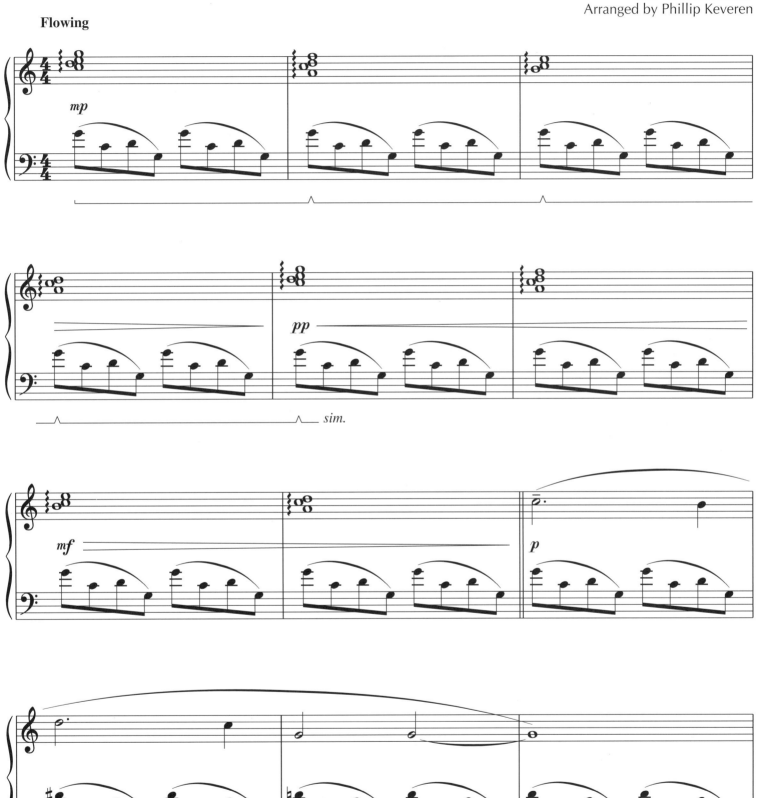

© Copyright 1943 by Gannon & Kent Music Co., Inc., Beverly Hills, CA
Copyright Renewed
This arrangement © Copyright 2001 by Gannon & Kent Music Co., Inc.
International Copyright Secured   All Rights Reserved

JINGLE BELLS

Words and Music by
J. PIERPONT
Arranged by Phillip Keveren

Copyright © 2001 by HAL LEONARD CORPORATION
International Copyright Secured   All Rights Reserved

LET IT SNOW! LET IT SNOW! LET IT SNOW!

Words by SAMMY CAHN
Music by JULE STYNE
Arranged by Phillip Keveren

Gently, with motion

Copyright © 1945 by Producers Music Publishing Co. and Cahn Music Co.
Copyright Renewed
This arrangement Copyright © 2001 by Producers Music Publishing Co. and Cahn Music Co.
All Rights for Producers Music Publishing Co. Administered by Chappell & Co.
All Rights for Cahn Music Co. Administered by WB Music Corp.
International Copyright Secured   All Rights Reserved

MERRY CHRISTMAS, DARLING

Words and Music by RICHARD CARPENTER
and FRANK POOLER
Arranged by Phillip Keveren

Copyright © 1970 IRVING MUSIC, INC.
Copyright Renewed
This arrangement Copyright © 2001 IRVING MUSIC, INC.
All Rights Reserved   Used by Permission

A MERRY CHRISTMAS TO ME

Words and Music by DAN RODOWICZ
and PHILLIP KEVEREN
Arranged by Phillip Keveren

Copyright © 1993 Cheldan Music and Kevko Music
This arrangement Copyright © 2001 Cheldan Music and Kevko Music
International Copyright Secured   All Rights Reserved

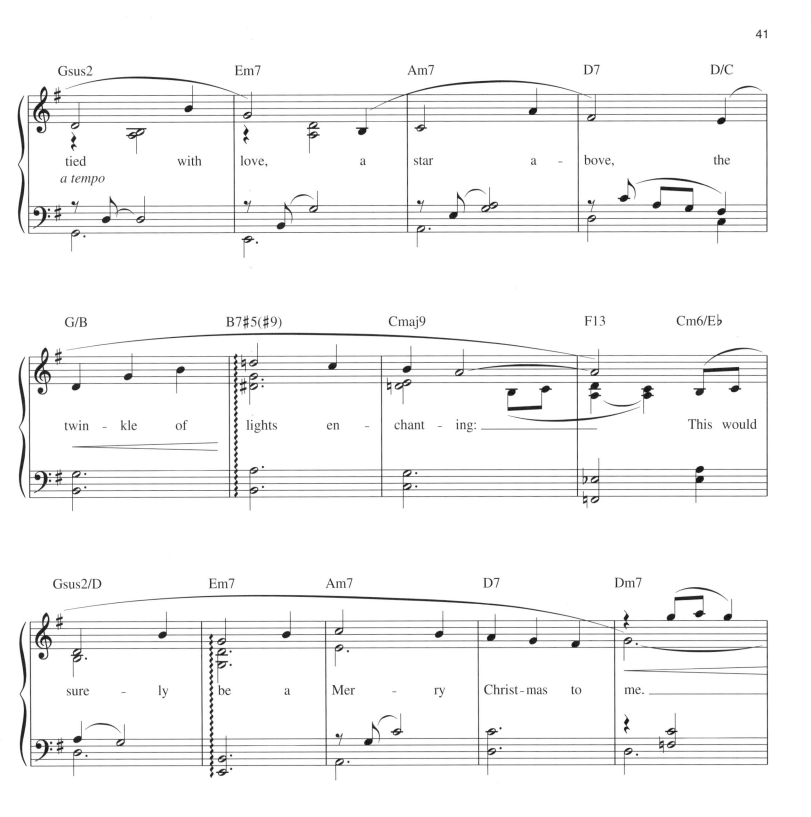

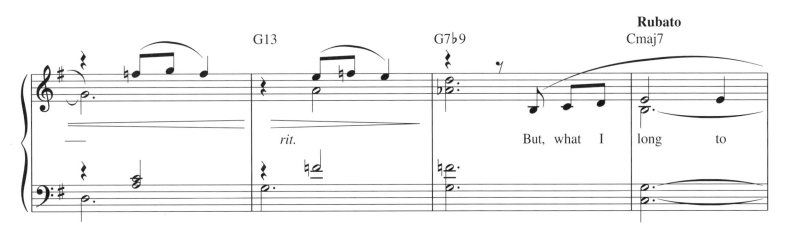

THE MOST WONDERFUL TIME OF THE YEAR

Words and Music by EDDIE POLA
and GEORGE WYLE
Arranged by Phillip Keveren

Light-hearted Waltz

Copyright © 1963 Barnaby Music Corp.
Copyright Renewed 1991
This arrangement Copyright © 2001 Barnaby Music Corp.
International Copyright Secured   All Rights Reserved

RUDOLPH THE RED-NOSED REINDEER

Music and Lyrics by
JOHNNY MARKS
Arranged by Phillip Keveren

Copyright © 1949 (Renewed 1977) St. Nicholas Music Inc., 1619 Broadway, New York, New York 10019
This arrangement Copyright © 2001 St. Nicholas Music Inc.
All Rights Reserved

Brisk Waltz

SILVER BELLS
from the Paramount Picture THE LEMON DROP KID

Words and Music by JAY LIVINGSTON
and RAY EVANS
Arranged by Phillip Keveren

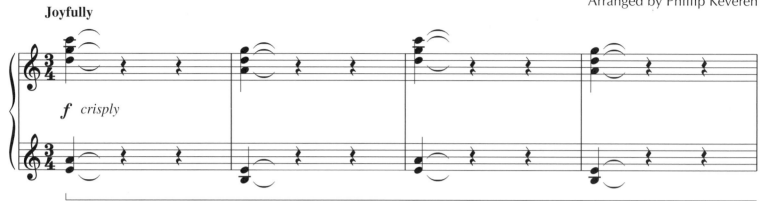

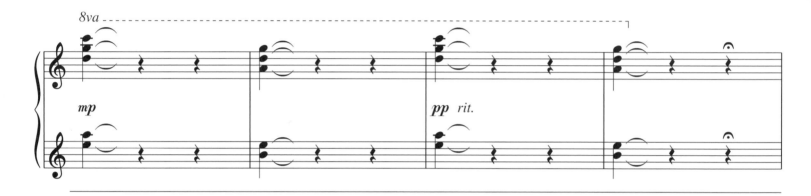

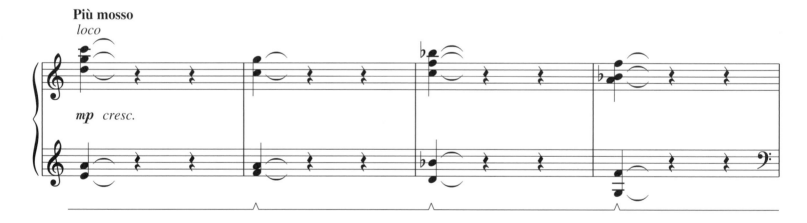

Copyright © 1950 (Renewed 1977) by Paramount Music Corporation
This arrangement Copyright © 2001 by Paramount Music Corporation
International Copyright Secured   All Rights Reserved

Moderate Waltz, with some rubato

SNOWFALL

Lyrics by RUTH THORNHILL
Music by CLAUDE THORNHILL
Arranged by Phillip Keveren

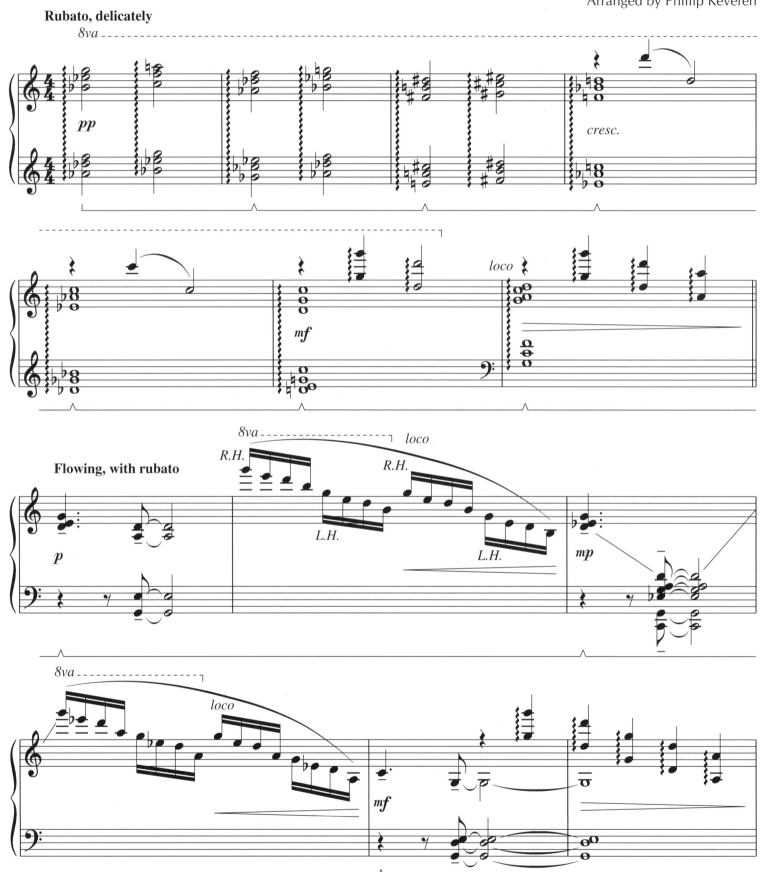

Copyright © 1941, 1968 by Chappell & Co.
Copyright Renewed
This arrangement Copyright © 2001 by Chappell & Co.
International Copyright Secured   All Rights Reserved

WE WISH YOU A MERRY CHRISTMAS

Traditional English Folksong
Arranged by Phillip Keveren

Brightly

Copyright © 2001 by HAL LEONARD CORPORATION
International Copyright Secured   All Rights Reserved

WHAT ARE YOU DOING NEW YEAR'S EVE?

By FRANK LOESSER
Arranged by Phillip Keveren

Rubato, warmly

© 1947 (Renewed) FRANK MUSIC CORP.
This arrangement © 2001 FRANK MUSIC CORP.
All Rights Reserved

Steady 4

No pedal

With pedal

f

rit. e dim.

pp

p